Measure
Your I.Q.

Other Titles of interest:

The Complete Book to Develop Your I.Q.
Succeed at I.Q. Tests

Measure
Your I.Q.

Gilles Azzopardi

foulsham

LONDON • NEW YORK • TORONTO • SYDNEY

foulsham
Yeovil Road, Slough, Berkshire SL1 4JH

ISBN 0-572-01935-1

This English language edition
copyright © 1993 W. Foulsham & Co. Ltd.

Originally published by:
Marabout, Alleur, Belgium © Marabout

Phototypeset in Great Britain by Typesetting Solutions, Slough, Berks.
Printed in Great Britain by Cox & Wyman Ltd., Reading.

CONTENTS

FOREWORD

In its original form, which is now obsolete, the intelligence quotient measured mental age in relation to chronological age.

Nowadays, we often refer to systems of intellectual valuation as the intelligence quotient. Usually, the scores achieved in a series of tests are added to 'standard' marks. According to the age of the person involved, these are then converted into an I.Q. with the help of different tables.

My method of calculating your I.Q. is similar to this. It allows you to assess your intellectual level as a whole, by using a unique table for all age groups.

Despite being fairly accurate, obviously this evaluation does not have the precision of a scientific test; mental ability cannot yet be measured like, for example, electrical current. Indeed, many people have been found to have varying I.Q. results, according to the method used to calculate them.

At present, the different intelligence scales used mean that individuals can only be categorised into large groups. For these reasons it is up to you to assess your own results, and perhaps make comparisons by taking other, similar tests.

MEASURE YOUR I.Q.

The following programme has been devised to allow you to rapidly assess your intelligence quotient, and estimate your intellectual output. There are four tests, each one consisting of 40 problems that you must solve, whilst at the same time rigidly adhering to the instructions given. These tests are preceded by a series of examples, devised to familiarise you with the type of problems presented.

Instructions

The results of these tests will only be valid if you obey the following instructions:

• The time allowed for each test is 30 minutes. When the 30 minutes have expired, you may no longer complete or correct your answers.

• You may, however, take as much time as you want to study the examples given and you can if you so wish, allow yourself a few minutes' break between each test.

• Dictionaries, calculators and similar aids are not allowed. All problems must be resolved in your mind, and the pen and paper you use is exclusively for writing down your answers.

• You must complete all four tests before checking your answers against the ones included in the book.

Some words of advice

• Normally it takes just over an hour to do these tests. Make sure you are relaxed, comfortable, and feeling intellectually bright before undertaking them. If necessary, disconnect the telephone or put on the answering machine so as not to be disturbed by any exterior sound or occurrence.

• You have 30 minutes per test to resolve 40 problems; that is to say, on average, less than a minute per problem. This means that you have no time to lose. Don't get stuck on one particular problem. If you cannot find the solution within a short period of time, move on to the next one.

• The best method is to resolve as many problems as you can within the shortest possible time, so that you can then go back to the more difficult ones, because it is almost impossible to solve all the problems within the time allowed. Do not worry, therefore, if at the end of the test you have not found all the solutions.

• One last piece of advice. Keep an alarm clock or stop-watch next to you while doing the tests to prevent worrying about the time.

• Do not re-read your answers while taking a quick break between tests; you might start doubting yourself, and that wouldn't help at all!

EXAMPLES

Examples* : Problems

These examples are designed to familiarise you with the sort of tests that follow. You may take as long as you like to study them, and compare your answers with those given.

1. **Which figure, of the six shown below, completes the sequence?**

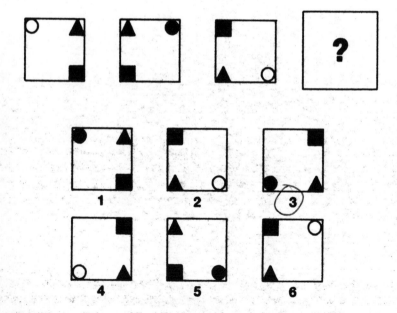

*All these problems are taken from *'Succeed at I.Q. Tests'* by the same author, in this series.

2. **Find a word which, when placed in the brackets, forms two different words with the letters outside the brackets? (synonym: *skill*).**

   P(. . .)ERY

3. **Which is the odd one out?**

   Lion   Tiger   Cat   Hyena   Panther

4. **Which letters go in the brackets?**

   EN(FORT)SU
   SH(. . . .)NF

5. **Which letter goes before the 4 to complete the sequence?**

   A1   D2   I3   R .4

6. **Which figure, of the 5 shown below, completes the sequence?**

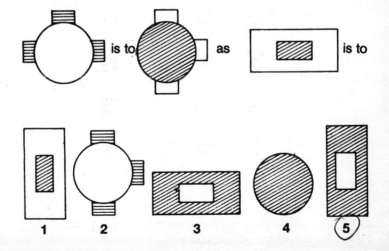

1   2   3   4   5

7. Which figure, of the 8 shown below, completes the sequence?

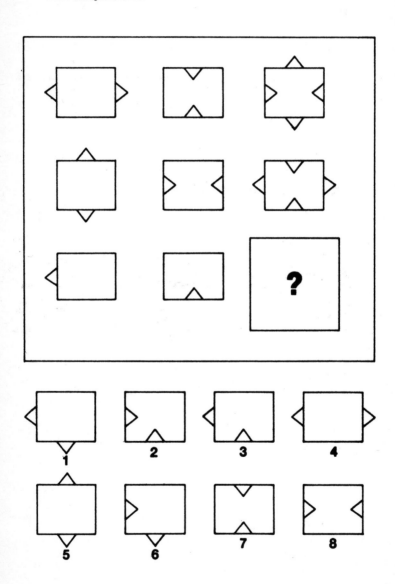

8. Complete the sequence.

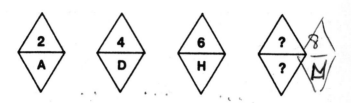

9. What is the missing number?

10. Fill in the missing domino to complete the sequence.

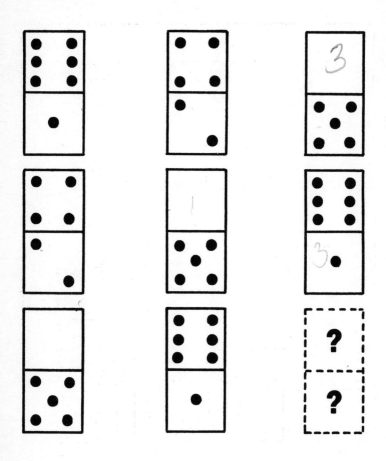

11. Which figure, of the 8 shown below, completes the sequence?

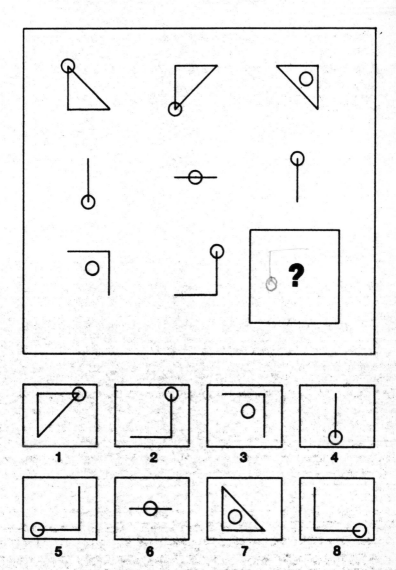

12. Which is the odd figure out?

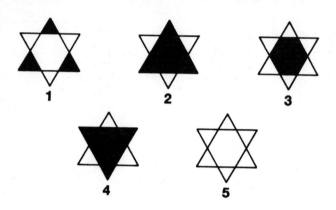

13. What are the missing numbers?

1	1	9	1	27	1	?
1	4	1	16	1	40	?

14. Which is the odd word out?

SORE
MELON
LUMP
RAPE

15. Which figure, of the six shown below, completes the sequence?

1   **2**   **3**

4   **5**   **6**

16. Which word completes the phrase?

'Clouds are to rain what lightning is to . . .'

Sky   *Wind*   *Thunder*   *Flash*   *Sunshine*

17. Complete the second line.

Jack   (Knave)   Rogue
Number   (.....)   Finger

18. Which word goes in the brackets to form two different words with the letters outside the brackets?

FORE(....)STRONG

19. What word goes in the brackets to form a different word with each letter?

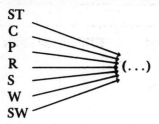

ST
C
P
R
S
W
SW
(...)

20. Fill in the missing domino.

Examples : Solutions

PROBLEM No.	SOLUTION	EXPLANATION
1		3 The circle and square move from corner to corner in a clockwise direction: the circle changes colour each time. The triangle moves anticlockwise.
2	ART	Forming the words PART and ARTERY.
3	HYENA	The only animal that isn't part of the cat family.
4	TIME	The word between the brackets is found, alphabetically, in this way: • 1st letter F comes after E outside the brackets. • 2nd letter O comes after N outside the brackets. • 3rd letter R comes before S outside the brackets. • 4th letter T comes before U outside the brackets. The same is true in the second line: T and I comes after S and H, M and E come before N and F.
5	P	The position of each letter in the alphabet corresponds to the number that goes with it, squared:, i.e.:

1^2 = A, 1st letter
2^2 = D, 4th letter
3^2 = I, 9th letter
4^2 = P, 16th letter.

6

5 The rectangle, like the circle, turns 90° clockwise, and the colours (grey and white) are reversed.

7

6 On each line, the right hand figure contains the number of triangles in the first two added together. The interior and exterior triangles are reversed.

8

The number in the top triangle goes up by 2 each time: 2 (+2=) 4 (+2=) 6 (+2=) 8. Each letter follows the one preceding it according to a simple alphabetical progression: D is the 3rd letter after A, H is the 4th after D, M the 5th after H.

9

88 The numbers in the 2nd circle are those in the 1st circle divided by 2. The numbers in the 3rd circle are those in the 1st circle, multiplied by 2.

10

4/2 Each line has the same three dominos, but in different positions.

11 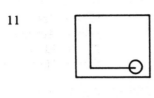 8 On each line, the figure turns 90° clockwise each time, and the circle has a different position each time: above, below or in the middle.

12  Figures 1 and 3, and 2 and 4, are opposites. Figure 5 does not have an opposite shown.

13 Starting with the top left hand square and alternating top and bottom, the number is obtained by adding together the preceding numbers from 3 onwards. 1 (+3=) 4 (+5=) 9 (+7=) 16 (+11=) 27 (+13=) 40 (+17=) 57. The 1 alternates between top and bottom.

14 SORE
ROSE
All four words are anagrams of plants. SORE is an anagram of ROSE, which is a flower. All the others are anagrams of trees.

15  6 The circles moves one place diagonally each time. The square moves one place to the left each time.

16 THUNDER Clouds come before rain, and lightning comes before thunder.

17	DIGIT	On each line the word in brackets is a synonym of the words outside the brackets.
18	HEAD	Which forms the words forehead and headstrong.
19	AGE	Which forms the words: stage, cage, page, rage, sage, wage and swage.
20	2/4	The value of the left hand side of the domino is formed by following the progression +2, −1: 1 is the 2nd number after 6, 0 is the 1st before 1, 2 the 2nd after 0, 1 the 1st before 2, 3 the 2nd after 1, 2 the first before 3. The value of the right hand side of the domino is formed by following the progression +1, +2, +3, +4, +5, +6: 5 is the 1st number after 4, 0 is the 2nd number after 5, 3 the 3rd number after 0, etc.

TEST I: PROBLEMS

1. Which figure, of the six shown below, completes the sequence?

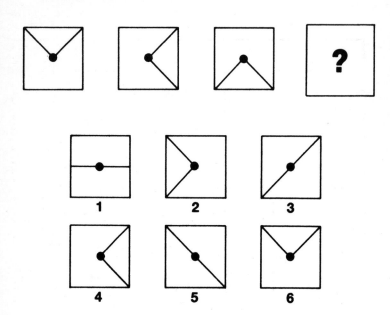

2. Which figure, of the eight numbered below, completes the sequence?

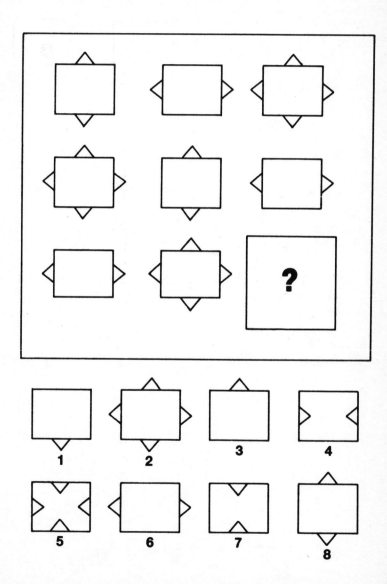

3. What is the missing number?

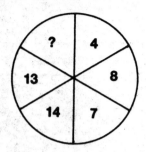

4. Which is the odd word out?

NATU
ICENE
CULEN
SARM
REFHAT

5. Which figure, of the six shown below, completes the sequence?

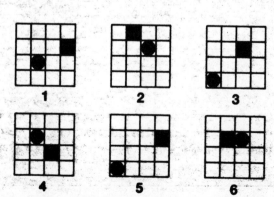

6. **Which figure, of the eight shown below, completes the sequence?**

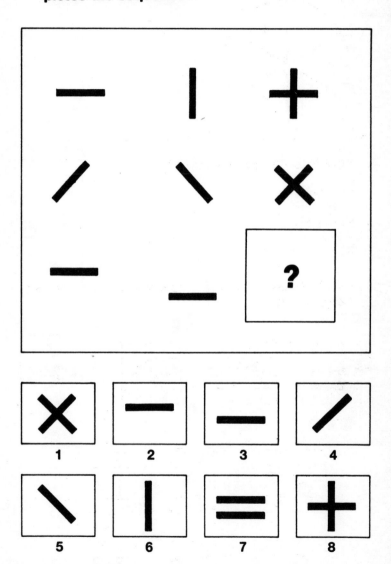

7. Fill in the missing domino.

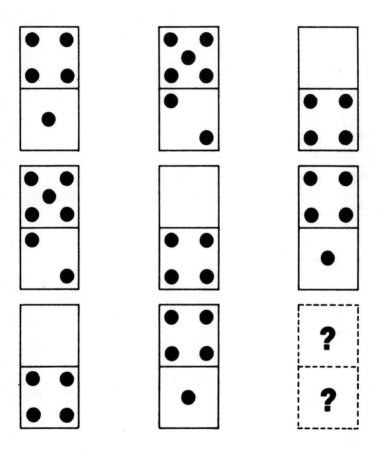

8. **Which figure, of the 5 shown below, completes the sequence?**

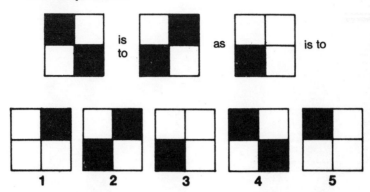

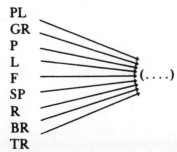

9. **Find a word which, when placed in the brackets, forms two different words with the letters outside the brackets. (synonym: *group*).**

   BAS(...)TER

10. **Find the letter that goes between the brackets to complete the sequence.**

    108 (O)   648 (S)   325 (T)   214(.)

11. **What word goes in the brackets?**

    Side   (Edit)   Yeti
    Over   (....)   Puts

12. **Find a word to go in the brackets which forms a different word with each letter(s) preceding it.**

    PL
    GR
    P
    L
    F   (....)
    SP
    R
    BR
    TR

13. Which figure, of the eight shown below, completes the sequence?

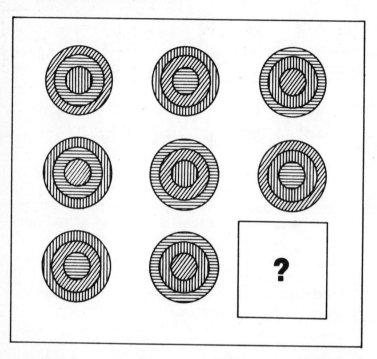

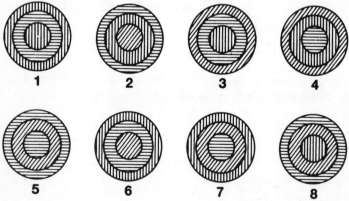

14. Which figure, of the 6 shown below, completes the sequence?

    1   2   3

    4   5   6

15. Find the missing number.

3	12	8
7	28	24
5	20	?

16. Find the missing letter.

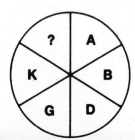

17. Which figure, of the 8 shown below, completes the sequence?

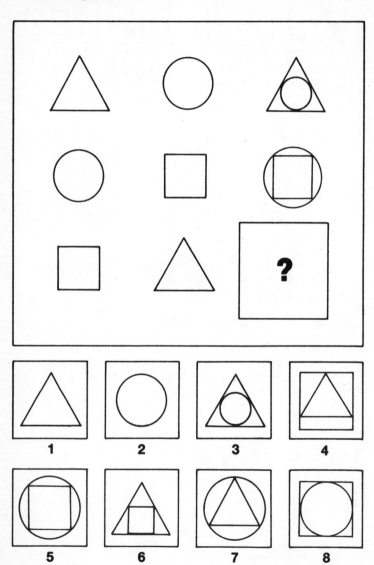

18. Which figure, of the 6 shown below, completes the sequence?

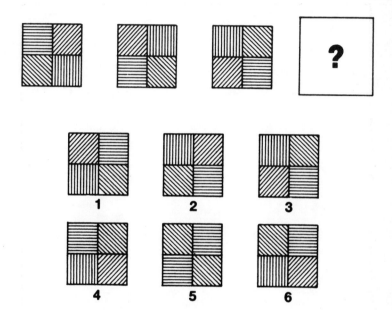

19. Which figure, of the 8 shown below, completes the sequence?

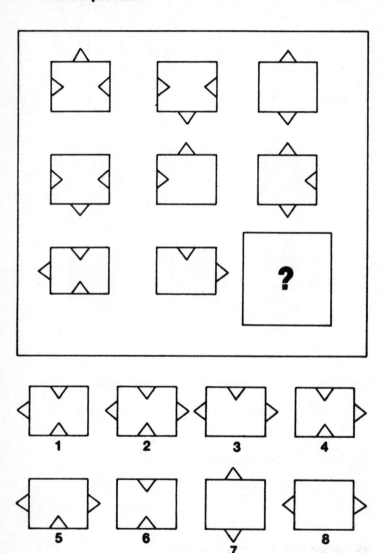

20. Which figure, of the 6 shown below, completes the sequence?

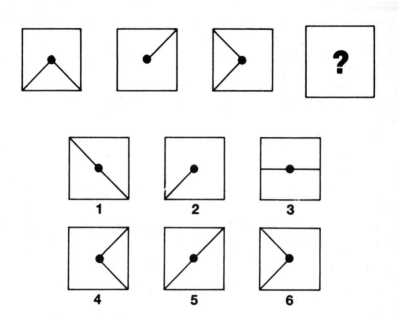

21. Which word completes the phrase?

Christmas trees are to Christmas what eggs are to . . .?

22. Find the missing number

326 (20) 432
427 (?)   113

23. What is the odd one out?

Chariot   Canapés   Croissant
Crionoline   Charabanc   Carafe

24. **What word goes in the brackets to form a different word with each letter(s) preceding it?**

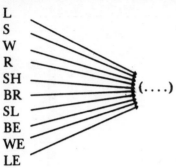

L
S
W
R
SH
BR
SL
BE
WE
LE

(. . . .)

25. **Which figure, of the 6 shown below, completes the sequence?**

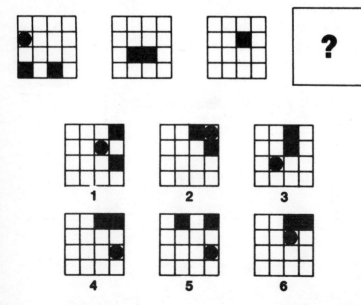

1

2

3

4

5

6

26. Which figure, of the 8 shown below, completes the sequence?

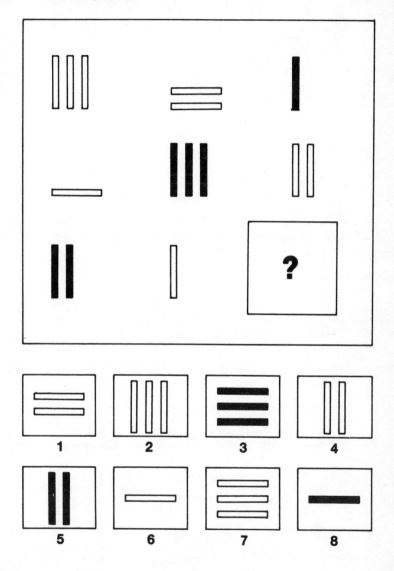

27. Find the missing numbers.

1	8	9	64	25	?	49
1	4	27	16	125	?	343

28. Which is the odd one out?

KYS
OMNO
NUVES
SARM
HARTE

29. Which figure, of the 6 shown below, completes the sequence?

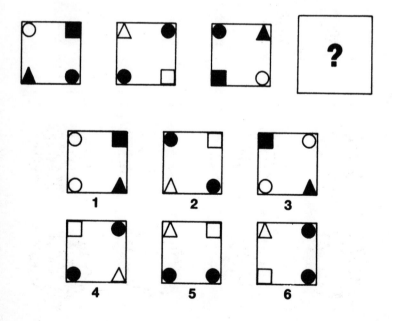

30. Which figure, of the 8 shown below, completes the sequence?

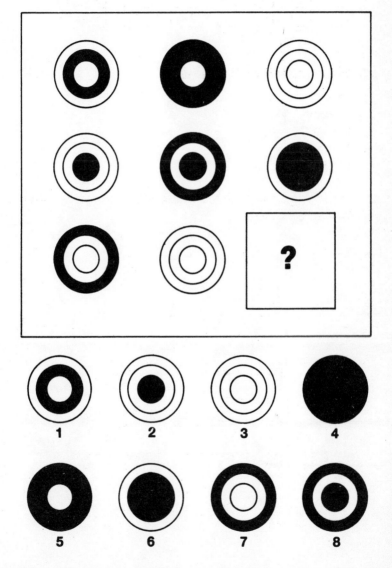

31. Fill in the missing domino.

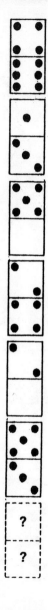

32. Which figure is the odd one out?

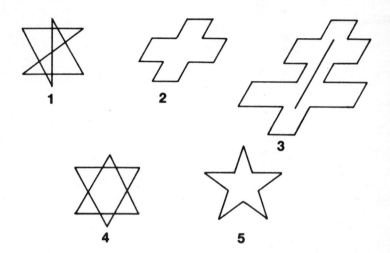

33. Find the missing letters or numbers.

E4   O2   M3   H1   HOME
A2   D5   I4   P3   R1 .....

34. What word goes in the brackets?

Zoo   (Zero)   Ersatz
Zulu   (....)   Ebony

35. Fill in the brackets on the second line.

Grumble   (Grouse)   Bird
Abandon   (......)   Colour

36. Find a word which, when placed in the brackets, forms two different words with the letters outside the brackets.

TOU(...)DLE

37. Which figure, of the 8 shown below, completes the sequence?

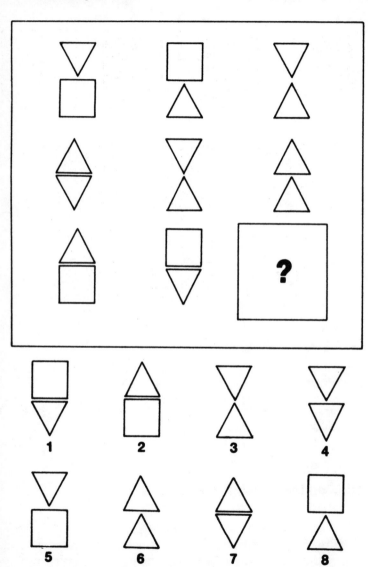

38. Which figure, of the 6 shown below, completes the sequence?

1   2   3

4   5   6

39. Find the missing letters.

40. Find the missing number.

TEST II: PROBLEMS

1. **Which figure, of the 6 shown below, completes the sequence?**

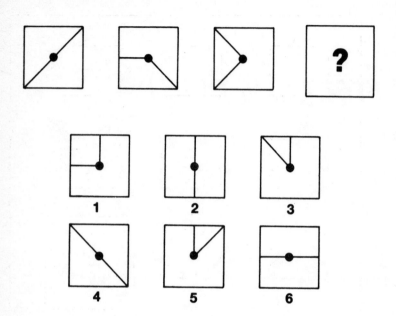

2. Which figure, of the 8 shown below, completes the sequence?

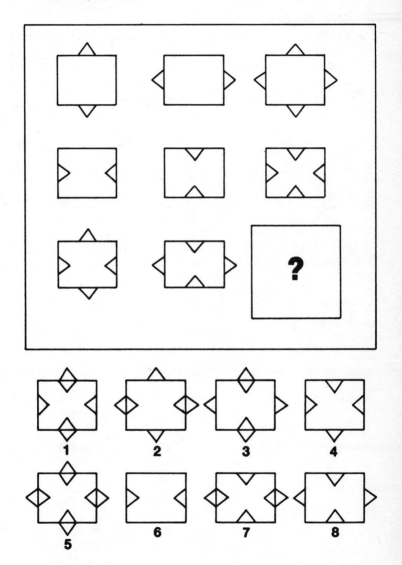

3. Which is the odd one out?

CLABK
OLLWEY
LUBE
NOIR
REPPUL

4. Find the missing numbers.

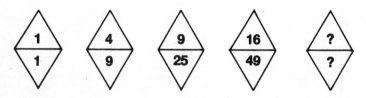

5. Which figure, of the 6 shown below, completes the sequence?

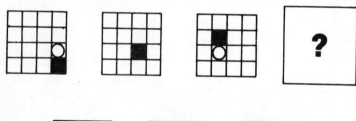

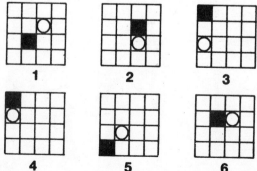

6. Which figure, of the 8 shown below, completes the sequence?

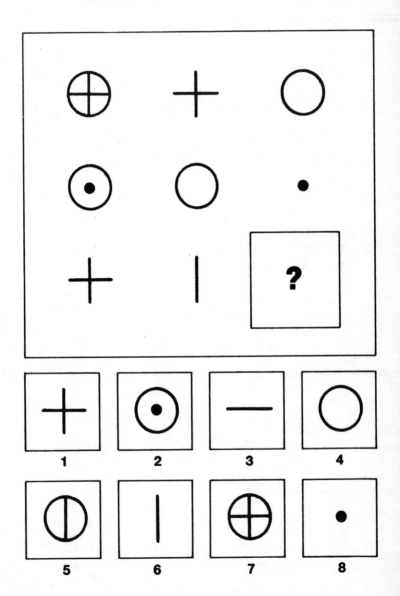

7. Fill in the missing domino.

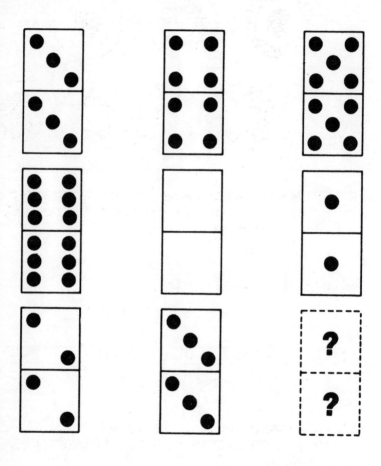

8. Which figure completes the sequence?

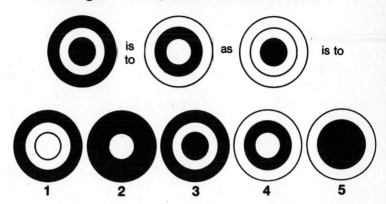

9. Find a word, which, when placed in the brackets, forms two different words with the letters outside the brackets. (synonym: *portion*).

RAM(. . . .)NER

10. Find the missing number.

Horse	Ass	Donkey	Hare
5	3	6	

11. What word goes in the brackets?

Ante	(Bode)	Beef
Chat	(. . . .)	Thou

12. Find a word, which when placed in the brackets forms a different word with each letter(s) preceding it.

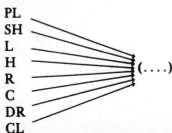

PL
SH
L
H
R
C
DR
CL

(. . . .)

13. Which figure completes the sequence?

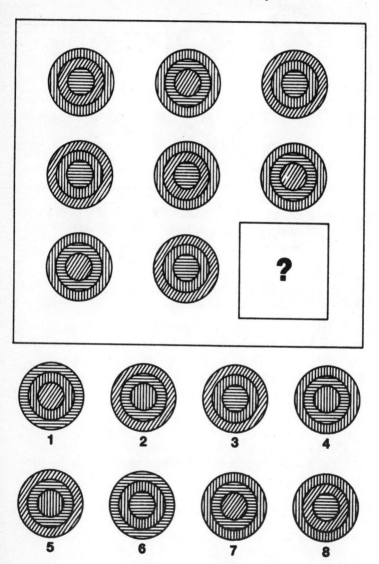

14. Which figure, of the 6 shown below, completes the sequence?

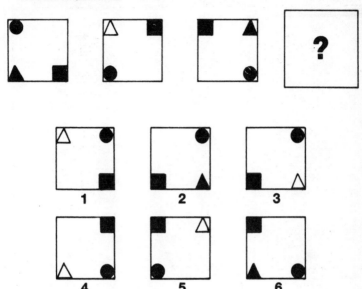

15. Find the missing letter.

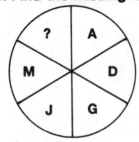

16. Find the missing number.

3	13	2
2	?	1
4	25	3

17. Which figure completes the sequence?

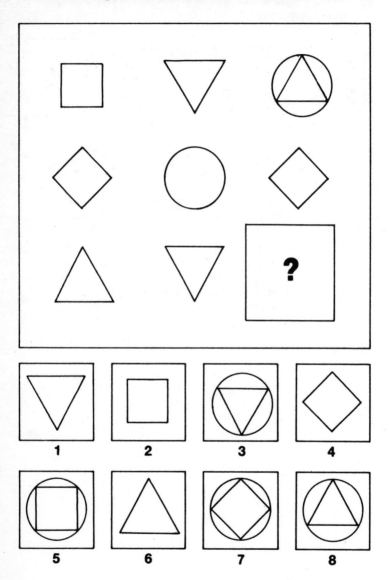

18. Which figure completes the sequence?

A	B
C	D

C	A
D	B

D	C
B	A

?	

A	C
D	B

1

B	D
C	A

2

A	D
C	B

3

C	B
D	A

4

B	D
A	C

5

D	C
B	A

6

19. Which figure completes the sequence?

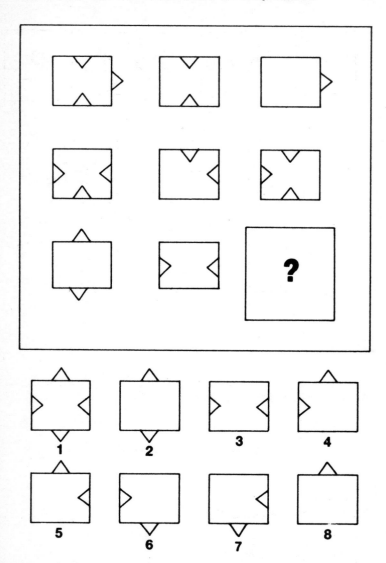

20. Which figure completes the sequence?

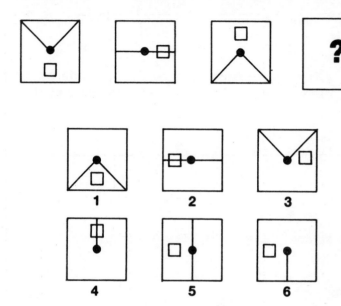

21. Complete the sentence.

'An oasis is to the desert what an island is to . . .'

the earth, the sky, heaven, hell, a fisherman, the sea

22. Find the missing number.

28   (82)   13
16   (?)   17

23. Which is the odd word out?

Circle   Triangle   Rectangle
Square   Cube   Diamond

24. What word, when placed in the brackets, forms a different word with each letter(s) preceding it?

J
CL
S   (....)
FL
P

25. Which figure completes the sequence?

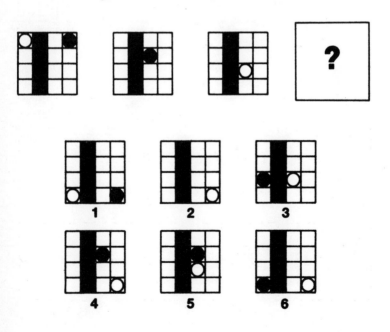

26. Which figure completes the sequence?

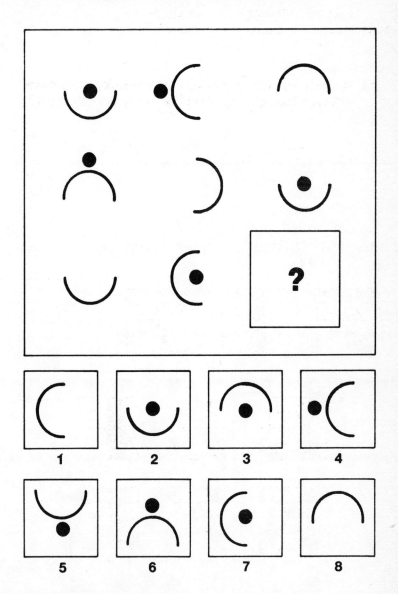

27. Find the missing number.

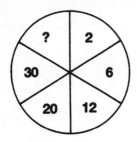

28. Which is the odd one out?

TOTAMO
CRAORT
MENLO
ELKE
RUNPTI

29. Which figure completes the sequence?

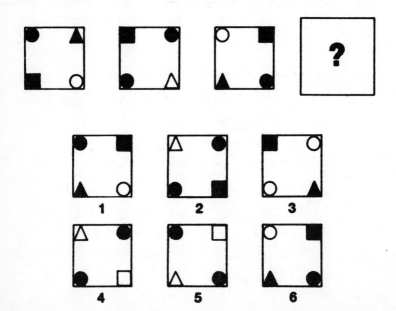

30. Which figure completes the sequence?

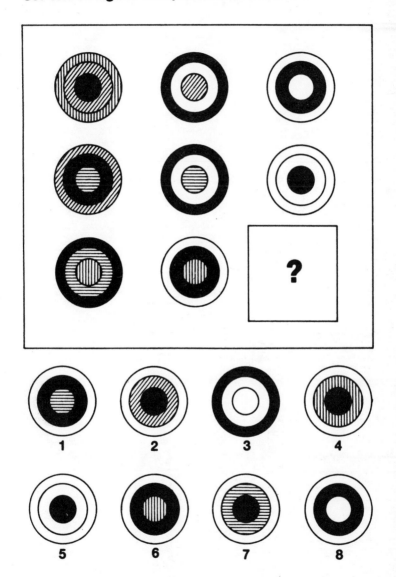

31. Fill in the missing dominos.

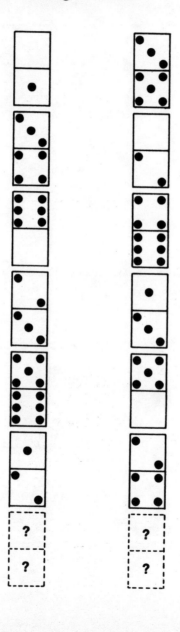

32. Which figure is the odd one out?

33. Find the missing number and letter.

5Y   4P   3I   2D   ..

34. What word goes in the brackets?

Ship   (Tide)   Reef
Snag   (....)   Hoof

35. Fill in the second line.

Grub   (Food)   Larva
Rope   (.....)   Telegram

36. What word goes in the brackets to form two different words with the letters outside the brackets?

CL(...)IC

37. Which figure completes the sequence?

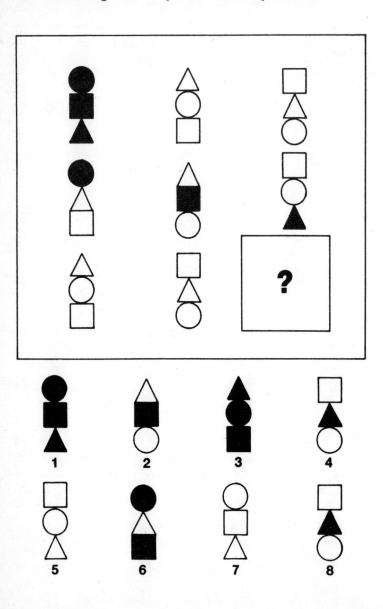

38. Which figure completes the sequence?

1

2

3

4   **5**   **6**

39. Find the missing number.

40. Find the missing letters.

A	X	E	?	I	P	M
Z	C	V	?	R	K	N

TEST III: PROBLEMS

1. Which figure completes the sequence?

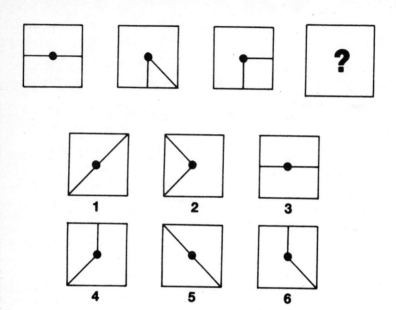

2. Which figure completes the sequence?

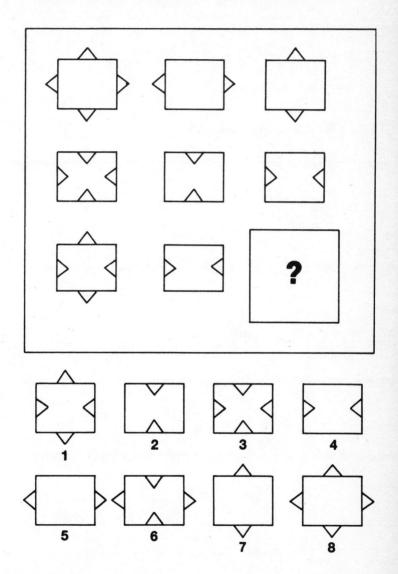

3. Find the missing numbers.

2	4	3	9	8	32	?
8	15	9	14	10	13	?

4. Which is the odd one out?

AUBERRFLY
FAYDIR
LIPRA
GAUSUT
BROCOTE

5. Which figure completes the sequence?

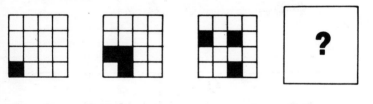

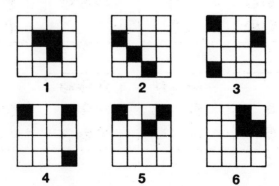

6. Which figure completes the sequence?

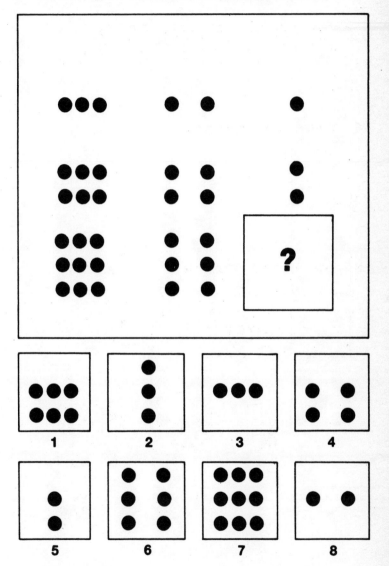

7. Fill in the missing domino.

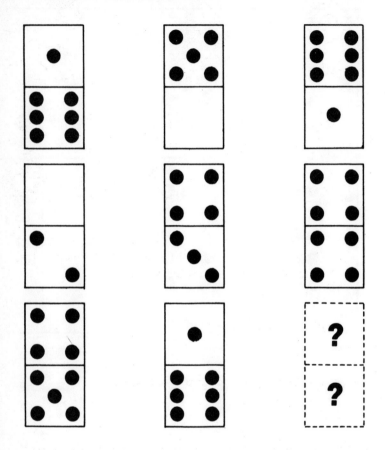

8. Which figure completes the sequence?

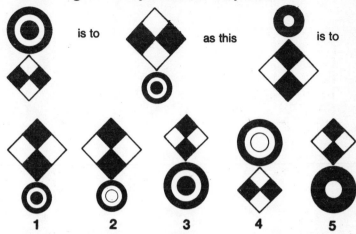

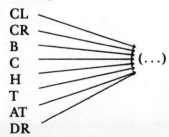

9. What word goes in the brackets to form two different words with the letters outside the brackets? (synonym: *insect*).

CLAIM(. . .)HILL

10. Find the next letter.

11   1   111   1111; E   O   H

11. What word goes in the brackets?

Obey	(Nabs)	Sect
Fog	(. . . .)	Set

12. Find a word which, when placed in the brackets forms a different word with each letter(s) preceding it.

CL
CR
B
C
H   (. . .)
T
AT
DR

13. Which figure completes the sequence?

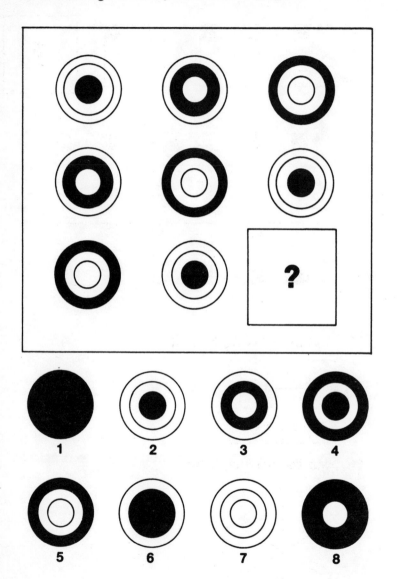

14. Which figure completes the sequence?

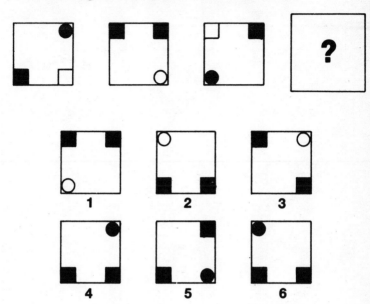

15. Find the missing number.

8	4	3	9
5	7	3	9
3	1	2	?

16. Find the missing letter.

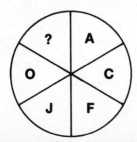

17. Which figure completes the sequence?

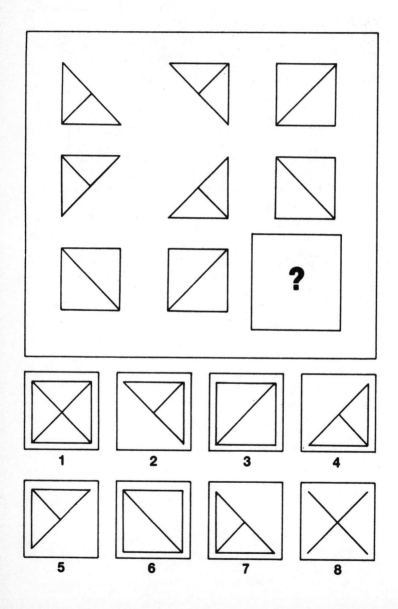

18. Which figure completes the sequence?

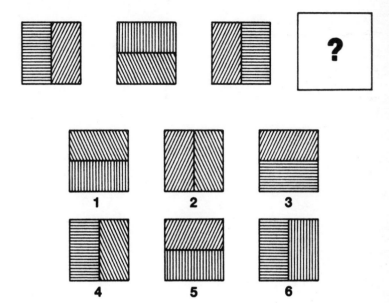

19. Which figure completes the sequence?

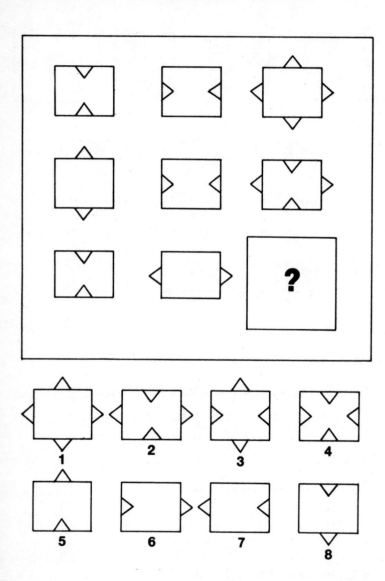

20. Which figure completes the sequence?

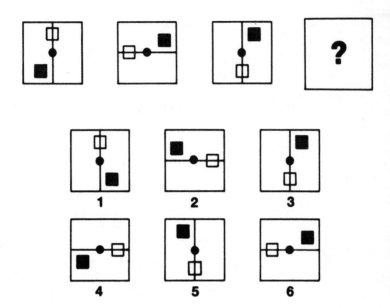

21. What word completes the sentence?

'Cheese is to a mouse what a carrot is to . . .'

an ox, a rabbit, a duck a chicken, a calf a lamb.

22. Find the missing number.

14 (7) 28
15 (?) 25

23. Which is the odd one out?

Eye   Ear   Cheek
Nose   Lip   Eyebrow

24. What word, when placed in the brackets, forms a different word with each letter(s) preceding it?

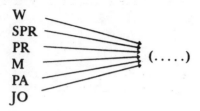

W
SPR
PR
M
PA
JO
(.....)

25. Which figure completes the sequence?

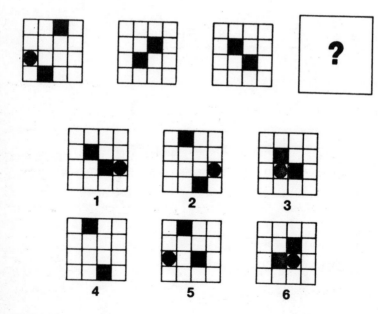

26. Which figure completes the sequence?

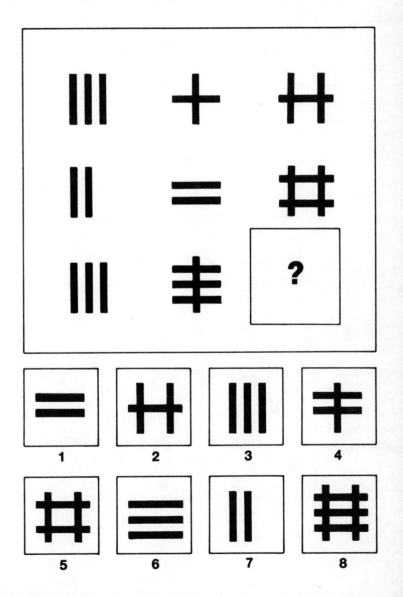

27. Which is the odd one out?

DANH
TOFO
GHITH
HURODSEL
CRICEL

28. Find the missing number.

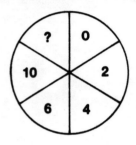

29. Which figure completes the sequence?

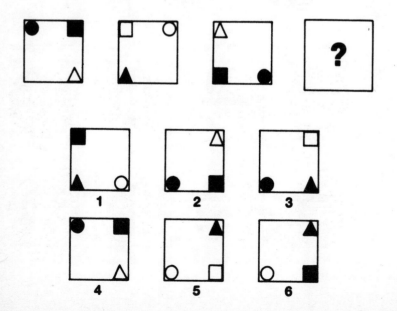

30. Which figure completes the sequence?

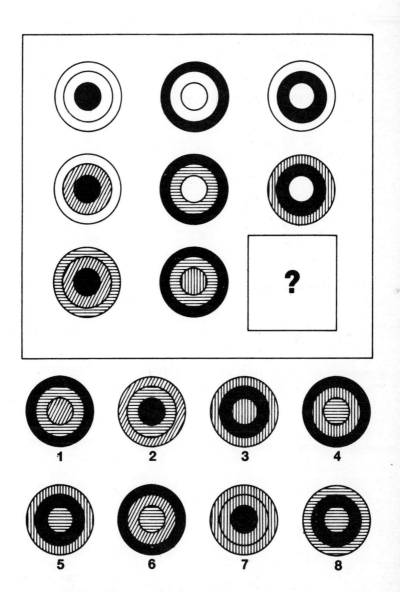

31. Fill in the missing domino.

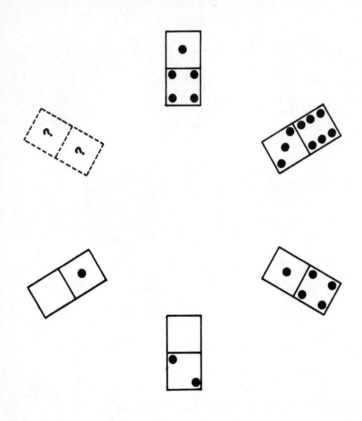

32. Which figure is the odd one out?

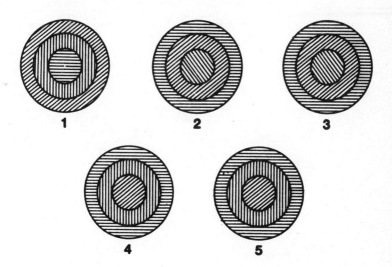

33. Find the missing letter.

22D   34L   53O   61.

34. What word goes in the brackets?

Star   (Tort)   Veto
Tear   (. . . .)   Came

35. What word goes in the brackets?

Hum   (Drone)   Bee
Only   (. . . .)   Fish

36. Which word, when placed in the brackets, forms two different words with the letters outside the brackets?

CAPS(. . .)GENT

37. Which figure completes the sequence?

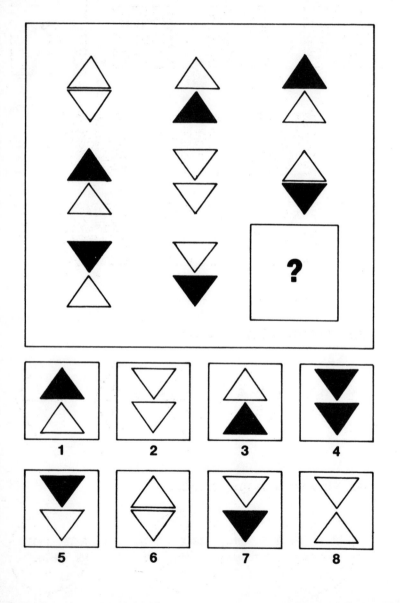

38. Which figure completes the sequence?

1   **2**   **3**

4   **5**   **6**

39. Find the missing letters.

40. Find the missing number.

TEST IV: PROBLEMS

1. Which figure completes the sequence?

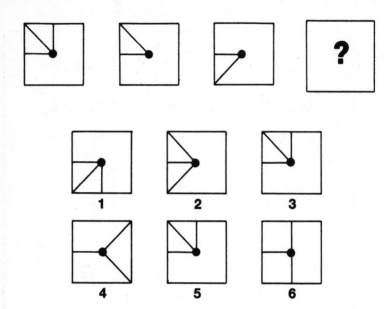

2. Which figure, of the 8 shown below, completes the sequence?

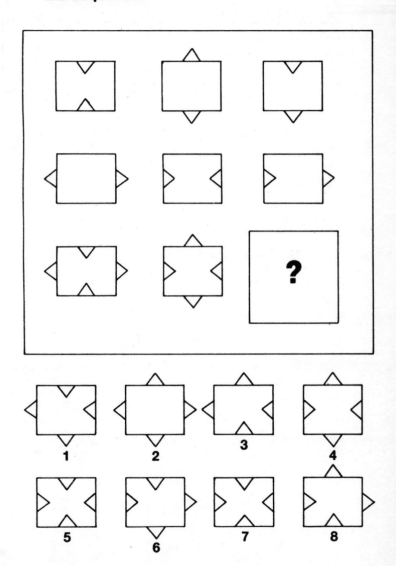

3. Which is the odd one out?

LUTIP
ONACRATIN
ONPYE
SORE
MEL

4. Find the missing numbers.

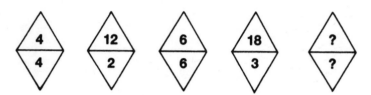

5. Which figure completes the sequence?

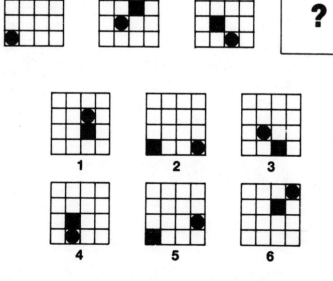

6. Which figure completes the sequence?

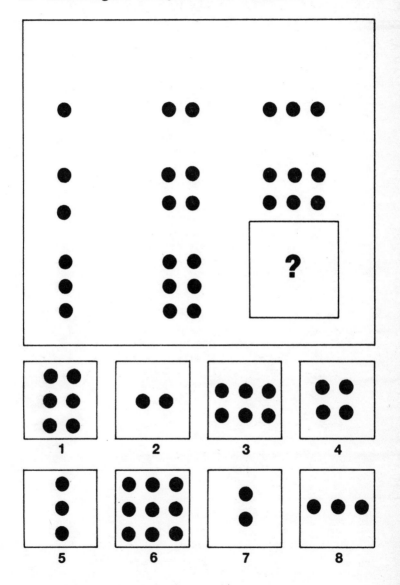

7. Fill in the missing domino.

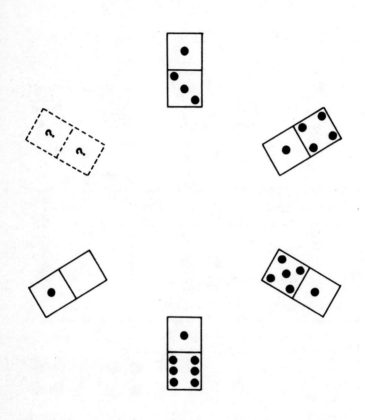

8. Which figure completes the sequence?

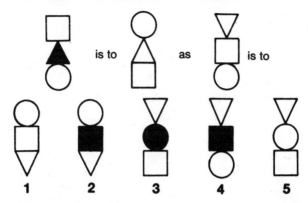

9. Find a word, which when placed in the brackets, forms two different words with the letters outside the brackets. (synonym: *decimal number*).

ROT(...)DON

10. Find the missing number.

IV3	II2	XII4	VIII5
XVI5	III3	V2	XIX.

11. What word goes in the brackets?

Pilot	(Late)	Place
Limit	(....)	Spine

12. Find a word which forms a different word with each preceding letter(s).

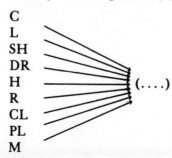

C
L
SH
DR
H   (....)
R
CL
PL
M

13. Which figure completes the sequence?

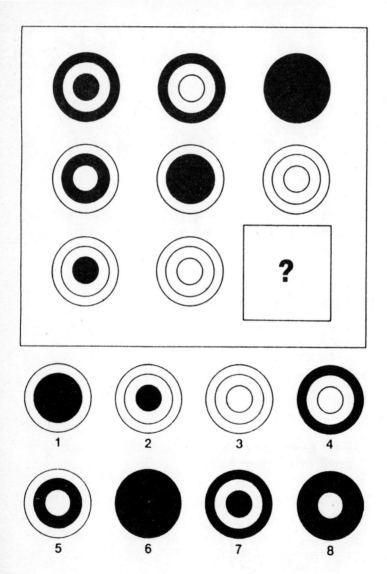

14. Which figure completes the sequence?

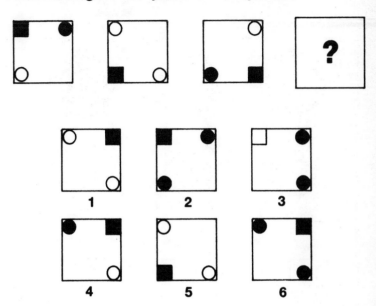

15. Find the missing number.

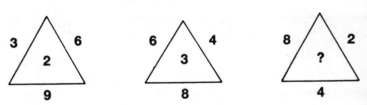

16. Which letters complete the sequence?

A	C	F	H	K	M	?
Z	Y	W	T	P	K	?

17. Which figure completes the sequence?

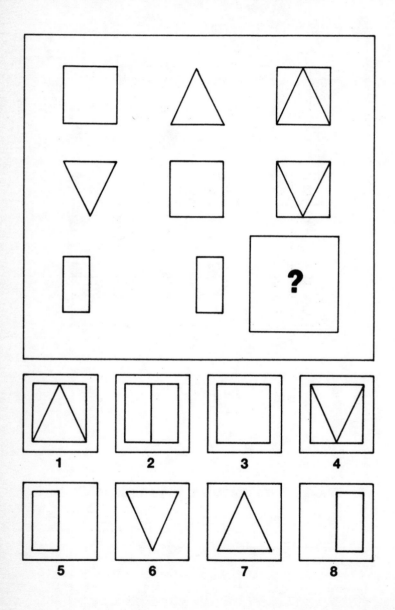

18. Which figure completes the sequence?

A	B
C	D

C	D
A	B

D	C
B	A

?

B	C
D	A

1

A	D
B	C

2

C	D
B	A

3

B	A
D	C

4

D	B
C	A

5

A	C
D	B

6

19. Which figure completes the sequence?

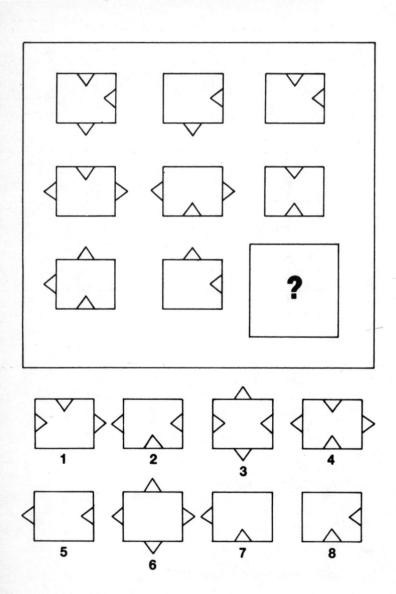

20. Which figure completes the sequence?

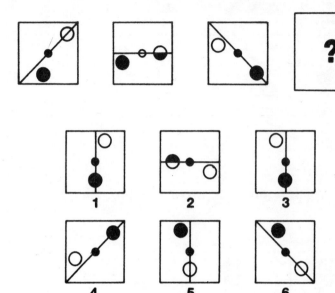

21. Complete the sentence.

'Wax is to bees what amber is to . . .'

slugs, sperm whales, tarragon, toads, sea-gulls, eels

22. Find the missing number.

23	(32)	41
47	(?)	31

23. Which is the odd one out?

Copper	Tin	Iron
Bronze	Lead	Aluminium

24. Find a word which forms a different word with
each preceding letter(s).

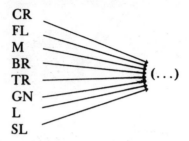

CR
FL
M
BR
TR
GN
L
SL

(...)

25. Which figure completes the sequence?

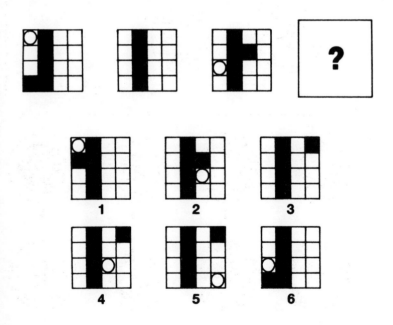

1   2   3

4   5   6

26. Which figure completes the sequence?

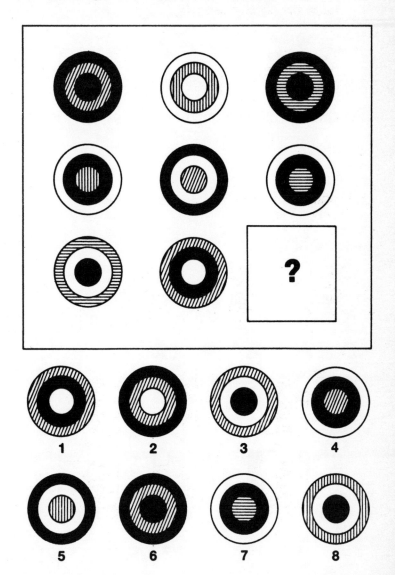

27. Which is the odd one out?

MANOYD
DAMDIY
SADUTEY
DARSAUTY
DHAYSTUR

28. Find the missing number.

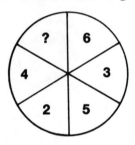

29. Which figure completes the sequence?

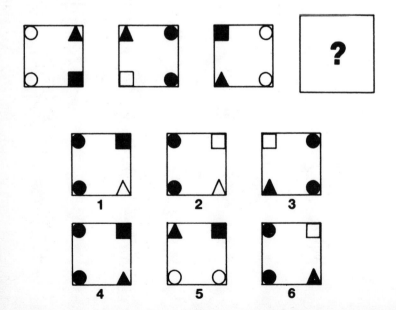

30. Which figure completes the sequence?

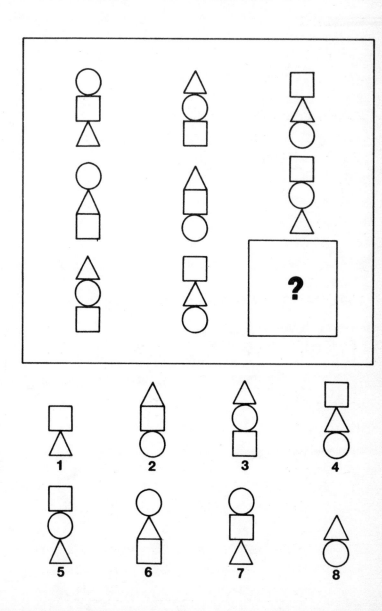

31. Fill in the missing domino.

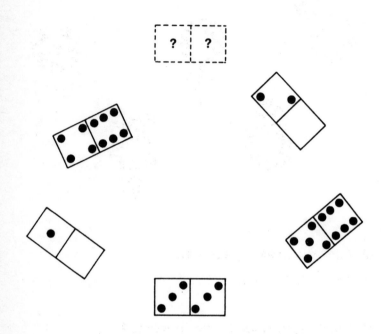

32. Which figure is the odd one out?

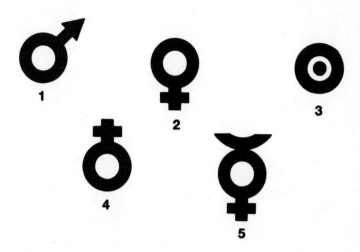

33. Find the missing number.

A43   C52   E61   G8.

34. What word goes in the brackets?

Kilt   (Look)   Polo
Log   (....)   Coca

35. What word goes in the brackets?

Smart   (Spruce)   Tree
Sweater (......)   Athlete

36. Find a word which, when placed in the brackets, forms two different words with the letters outside the brackets.

LAND(....)BIRD

37. Which figure completes the sequence?

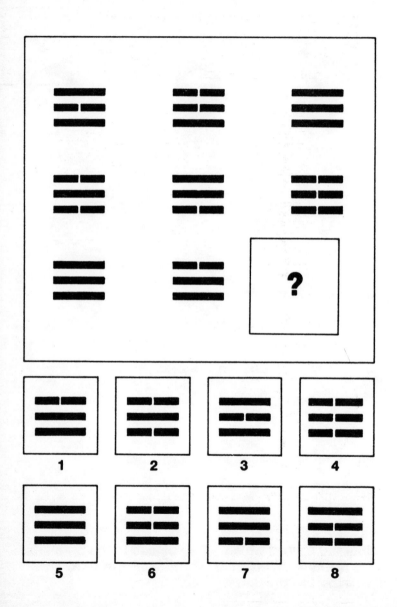

38. Which figure completes the sequence?

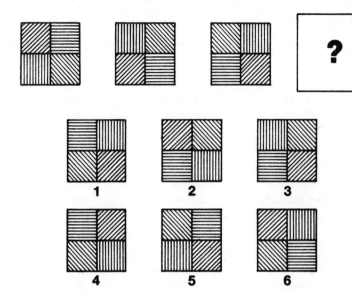

39. Find the missing letter.

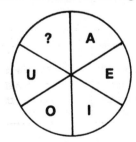

40. Find the missing number.

8	5	11
13	?	4
3	12	9

TEST I: SOLUTIONS

PROBLEM No.	SOLUTION	EXPLANATION
1	2	The two lines inside the square move 90° clockwise each time.
2	8	Each horizontal line has the same three figures in a different order.
3	26	4, 8, 7, 14, 13 ... 26. The sequence progresses in the form of $\times 2$, -1. $4 (\times 2=) 8 (-1=) 7 (\times 2=) 14 (-1=) 13 (\times 2=) 26$.
4	MARS	All are anagrams of relatives, except 'MARS'. Aunt, Niece, Uncle, Father.
5	5	The circle moves diagonally from top to bottom; the square moves horizontally from left to right.
6	7	On each line, the right hand figure is a combination of the two preceding it.
7		On each line, there are the same three dominos in a different order.

PROBLEM No.	SOLUTION	EXPLANATION
8		5 Each figure turns 90° clockwise in relation to the first.
9	SET	Which makes the names of two types of dog, BASSET and SETTER.
10	T	The letter that follows each number is the first letter of the number when written out in full.
11	REST	On each line, the first two letters of the word in brackets are the last two letters of the word to the left of it; the last two letters are the last from that to the right of it. The two letters are reversed each time.
12	ACED	Which forms the words: placed, graced, paced, laced, faced, spaced, raced, braced and traced.
13		3 Each figure is composed of three patterns: vertical, horizontal and diagonal stripes. On each line, the patterns are repeated in a different order.

PROBLEM No.	SOLUTION	EXPLANATION
14	2	The square and the triangle turn 90° clockwise each time. The circle turns 90° anti-clockwise each time.
15	16	On each line, the right hand number is obtained by multiplying it by 4 and then subtracting 4. 3 (×4=) 12 (−4=) 8 7 (×4=) 28 (−4=) 22 5 (×4=) 20 (−4=) 16
16	P	B is the 1st letter after A. D is the 2nd letter after B. G is the 3rd letter after D. K is the 4th letter after G. P is the 5th letter after K.
17	4	On each line, the right hand figure is obtained by superimposing the two preceding it; the second one is enclosed by the first.
18	6	Each figure turns 90° clockwise from the one preceding it.

PROBLEM No.	SOLUTION	EXPLANATION

19

5 On each line, the right hand figure is obtained by superimposing the two preceding it. The interior triangles cancel each other out when situated in the same position, whereas any exterior triangles remain.

20

5 The left hand line turns 180° clockwise each time. The right hand line turns 90° anti-clockwise each time.

21   Easter

Christmas trees are to Christmas as eggs are to Easter.

22   18

The number in brackets is obtained by adding up each number outside the brackets:
3+2+6+4+3+2 = 20.
4+2+7+1+1+3 = 18.

23   Crinoline

The only word in the sequence that does not contain the letter A.

24   AVER

Which forms the words: laver, saver waver, raver, shaver, braver, slaver, beaver, weaver and leaver.

25

4 The circle moves diagonally, one down, one up, each time. The left hand square moves diagonally upwards each time. The

PROBLEM No.	SOLUTION	EXPLANATION

right hand square moves vertically upwards each time.

26

7 Each line contains the same three figures in a different arrangement. One of these figures is in black. The white figures are alternately vertical and horizontal.

27

Starting with the top left hand square, and alternating top and bottom, the numbers are obtained in this way:
$(1^2=)$ 1 $(2^2=)$ 4 $(3^2=)$ 9 $(4^2=)$ 16 $(5^2=)$ 25 $(6^2=)$ 36 $(7^2=)$ 49.
The bottom left hand square starts a second series, which also alternates between top and bottom, but this time it is cubed:
$(1^3=)$ 1 $(2^3=)$ 8 $(3^3=)$ 27 $(4^3=)$ 63 $(5^3=)$ 125 $(6^3=)$ 216 $(7^3=)$ 343.

28   SKY

All the others are planets: MOON, VENUS, MARS, EARTH.

29

4 The white circle, the square and the triangle turn 90° clockwise, and change colour each time.

PROBLEM No.	SOLUTION		EXPLANATION
			The black circle also moves 90° clockwise each time, but without changing colour.
30		5	On each line, the exterior ring changes colour each time. The middle ring changes colour every second time, and the inner ring remains the same colour all the time.
31		1/6	Working from the FOUR of the middle domino, the numbers on the dominos going downwards are identical to the numbers on the dominos going upwards, and the FOUR at the top balances the FOUR in the middle.
32		1	The only figure containing a right-angle.
33	RAPID		The numbers following the letters give the position of that particular letter in the word.
34	ZEBU		The first and last letters of the word in brackets are the first and last letters of the word on the left. The middle two letters are the first two letters of the word on the right.

PROBLEM No.	SOLUTION	EXPLANATION
35	MAROON	A synonym of 'abandon' and 'colour'.
36	CAN	Which forms the words TOUCAN and CANDLE.
37	7	The right hand figure is composed of the top and bottom parts of the two figures preceding it.
38	6	The right hand side of the figure alternates between horizontal and vertical stripes. The left hand side of the figure turns 45° anti-clockwise each time.
39		In the top triangle, the letters progress in the form of A B C D ... E and C D E F ... G. In the bottom triangle, each letter is separated from the one that precedes it by 1, then 2, 3, 4 letters of the alphabet back to front: Z(y) X(wv) U(tsr) Q(ponm) L.

PROBLEM No.	SOLUTION	EXPLANATION
40	8	In each circle, the bottom number is obtained by dividing the number on the left by the number on the right, then dividing the result by 2. $14/7 = 2 \ (\times 2) = 4$ $18/3 = 6 \ (\times 2) = 12$ $12/3 = 4 \ (\times 2) = 8$.

TEST II: SOLUTIONS

PROBLEM No.	SOLUTION	EXPLANATION

1

3 The lower left hand line turns 45° clockwise each time. The top right hand line turns 90° clockwise each time.

2

5 On each line, the right hand figure is obtained by superimposing the two figures preceding it.

3

IRON (NOIR)

When the anagrams are resolved, IRON is the only metal amongst colours: BLACK, YELLOW, BLUE and PURPLE.

4

In the top triangle it is a sequence of 1^2, 2^2, 3^2, 4^2, 5^2:
$(1^2=)$ 1 $(2^2=)$ 4 $(3^2=)$ 9 $(4^2=)$ 16 $(5^2=)$ 25.
In the lower triangle, it is a sequence of odd numbers squared:
$(1^2=)$ 1 $(3^2=)$ 9 $(5^2=)$ 25 $(7^2=)$ 49 $(9^2=)$ 81.

5

3 The circles moves horizontally one place each time, from right to left. The square moves diagonally one place each time, from bottom to top.

PROBLEM No.	SOLUTION	EXPLANATION
6	3	On each line, the right hand figure is obtained by superimposing the two figures preceding it. Two identical shapes cancel each other out.
7		The right hand domino on each line is simply the next double from those preceding it.
8	2	The second figure of each pair is the opposite of the one preceding it.
9	PART	Which forms the words RAMPART & PARTNER.
10	4	The number below each word is given by the number of letters in the word.
11	DINT	The word in brackets is formed in this way: the first two letters come from the two letters that follow, in the alphabet, the first two letters of the left hand word (O after N, like B after A, and I after H, like D after E. The last two letters come from the two letters that

PROBLEM No.	SOLUTION	EXPLANATION
		precede, in the alphabet, the last two letters of the right hand word (D before E and E before F like N and T before O and U).
12	OVER	Which forms the words: plover, shover, lover, hover, rover, cover, drover and clover.
13	8	Each circle contains three different patterns, and in each line the pattern in the middle ring changes with each circle.
14	3	The circle and square move 45° anti-clockwise each time. The triangle moves 45° clockwise and changes colour each time.
15	P	Each letter is separated from the one preceding it by two letters: A (bc) D (ef) G (hi) J (kl) M (no) P.
16	5	On each line, the middle number is obtained by adding together the squares of the numbers to the left and right of it:

PROBLEM No.	SOLUTION	EXPLANATION

$$3^2 + 2^2 = \ 9 + 4 = 13$$
$$4^2 + 3^2 = 16 + 9 = 25$$
$$2^2 + 1^2 = \ 4 + 1 = \ 5.$$

17

5 The right hand figure on each of the two diagonal lines is obtained by superimposing the two figures preceding it. The circle encloses the square, just as it does the triangle in the top right hand figure.

18

B	D
A	C

5 Each letter moves one place clockwise each time.

19

1 On each line, the right hand figure is obtained by superimposing the two figures preceding it. Identical shapes cancel each other out.

20

6 The right hand arm turns 45° clockwise each time. The left hand arm turns 45° anti-clockwise each time. The small square moves 90° anti-clockwise each time.

21   SEA

An oasis is to the desert what an island is to the sea.

22   66

The number in brackets is obtained by adding to-

PROBLEM No.	SOLUTION	EXPLANATION

gether the two numbers each side of the brackets, and multiplying this by 2: $28 + 13 = 41 \times 2 = 82$. $16 + 17 = 33 \times 2 = 66$.

| 23 | CUBE | The only volume amongst a series of flat figures. |

| 24 | AWED | Which forms the words: jawed, clawed, sawed, flawed and pawed. |

25 — 6 The white circle moves one place diagonally each time from top to bottom, left to right. The black circle moves one place diagonally from top to bottom, right to left.

26 — 6 On each line, the curve turns 90° clockwise each time. The dot is alternately inside, outside and absent.

27 — 42 — The sequence is 2, 3, 4, 5, 6 7, all squared, minus 2, 3, 4, 5, 6 and 7:
$(2^2-2=)$ 2 $(3^2-3=)$ 6
$(4^2-4=)$ 12 $(5^2-5=)$ 20
$(6^2-6=)$ 30 $(7^2-7=)$ 42.

28 — LEMON (MENLO) — WHen the anagrams are resolved, lemon is the only citrus fruit amongst vegetables: TOMATO, CARROT, LEEK and TURNIP.

PROBLEM No.	SOLUTION		EXPLANATION

29
2 The square and the triangle move 90° clockwise each time, with the triangle changing colour. The two circles move 90° anti-clockwise, with the white circle changing colour.

30
5 On each line, the first figure contains three patterns, the second figure contains two patterns, and the third figure, one pattern. The black pattern alternates between being the exterior, middle and interior circle on each line.

31   4/5   6/1
In the left hand column the numbers on each domino are consecutive but there is a gap of one unit between the dominos. Thus: 0/1 (2) 3/4 (5) 6/0 (1) 2/3 (4) 5/6 (0) 1/2 (3) 4/5. The dominos in the right hand column are also separated by a one unit gap, but this time the numbers on each domino are also separated by one unit. Thus: [3(4)5] (6) [0(1)2] (3) [4(5)6] (0) [1(2)3] (4) [5(6)0] (1) [2(3)4] (5) [6(0)1].

32
The only triangle that does not contain any vowels.

PROBLEM No.	SOLUTION	EXPLANATION
33	1A	The number before each letter corresponds to its position in the alphabet when squared: Y, 25th letter = 5^2. P, 16th letter = 4^2. I, 9th letter = 3^2. D, 4th letter = 2^2. A, 1st letter = 1^2.
34	TONE	The word in brackets is formed in this way. The first two letters come from the two letters that follow, alphabetically, the first two letters of the left hand word (T and O follow S and N like T and I follow S and H on the first line). The last two letters come from the two letters that precede, alphabetically, the last two letters of the right hand word.
35	CABLE	A synonym of ROPE and TELEGRAM.
36	ASP	Which forms the words CLASP and ASPIC.
37		1 On each line there are the same three shapes in a different order. The square is black when it is in the centre, as is the circle when it is at the top, and the triangle when it is at the bottom.

PROBLEM No.	SOLUTION	EXPLANATION

38

5 In the left hand side of the square, the pattern is alternately horizontal and vertical. On the right, the pattern is alternately left diagonals and right diagonals.

39

2   1
   6
   9

The number inside the triangle is obtained by multiplying together the numbers outside it, and dividing that by 3:
$4 \times 3 \times 2 = 24 \div 3 = 8$
$3 \times 5 \times 6 = 90 \div 3 = 30$
$2 \times 1 \times 9 = 18 \div 3 = 6$.

40

T
G

Starting with A (top left) and alternating top and bottom, each letter is separated by one letter of the alphabet: A (b) C (d) E (f) G (h) I (j) K (l) M. The same applies to Z (bottom left), this time with the alphabet going backwards: Z (y) X (w) V (u) T (s) R (q) P (o) N.

TEST III: SOLUTIONS

PROBLEM No.	SOLUTION	EXPLANATION
1		4 The left hand arm moves 90° anti-clockwise each time. The right hand arm 45° clockwise each time.
2		7 On each line, the right hand figure is obtained by superimposing the two preceding it. Identical shapes cancel each other out.
3	**31** **11**	In the top square, the sequence is: ×2 −1, ×3 −1, ×4 −1, etc. 2 (×2=) 4 (−1=) 3 (×3=) 9 (−1=) 8 (×4=) 32 (−1=) 31. In the bottom square, the sequence is: +7, −6, +5, −4, +3, −2. 8 (+7=) 15 (−6=) 9 (+5=) 14 (−4=) 10 (+3=) 13 (−2=) 11.
4	FRIDAY (FAYDIR)	The only day among the months FEBRUARY, APRIL, AUGUST and OCTOBER.
5		4 The squares move one place vertically, one place diagonally and one place horizontally each time.

PROBLEM No.	SOLUTION	EXPLANATION

6   2   Each figure is increased on each line by a repitition of the top line of that column.

7   5/0   On each line, the top half of the right hand domino is obtained by adding together the top halves of the preceding two. 1 + 5 = 6, 0 + 4 = 4, 4 + 1 = 5.

The bottom half is obtained by following the sequence 6, 0, 1, 2, 3, 4, 5, 6, 0.

8   5   The second figure of each pair contains the same shapes as the one preceding it, but their position and size are reversed.

9   ANT   Which forms the words: **CLAIMANT AND ANTHILL.**

10   T   The letters represent the first letter of each number when written out in full.

11   ENDS   The first two letters of the word in brackets precede, alphabetically, the first two letters of the

PROBLEM No.	SOLUTION	EXPLANATION

word to the left. N and A precede O and B, just as E and N precede F and O. The last two letters of the word in brackets precede, alphabetically, the last two letters of the word to the right. B and S precede C and T, just as D and S precede E and T.

12   ONES

Which forms the words: clones, crones, bones, cones hones tones, atones and drones.

13

3 On each line there are the same three figures, but in a different order.

14

2 The white square moves 90° anti-clockwise and changes colour each time. The black square and the circle move 90° clockwise, with the circle changing colour each time.

15   2

On each line, the right hand number is obtained by adding together the first two numbers and subtracting the third:
$8 + 4 - 3 = 9$
$5 + 7 - 3 = 9$
$3 + 1 - 2 = 2$

PROBLEM No.	SOLUTION	EXPLANATION
16	U	Each letter is separated from the one preceding it by 1, then 2, then 3, 4 and 5 letters alphabetically: A (b) C (de) F (ghi) J (klmn)) (pqrst) U.
17		8 The right hand figure is obtained by superimposing the first two figures and erasing any identical lines these two figures contain.
18		1 The complete figure turns 90° clockwise each time.
19		3 On each line, the right hand figure is obtained by superimposing the two preceding figures and inverting the triangles: exterior triangles become interior and vice-versa.
20		4 The line and the white square move 90° anticlockwise each time. The black square also moves 90° anti-clockwise, but alternates from one side of the line to the other.
21	A RABBIT	Cheese is to a mouse what carrot is to a rabbit.

PROBLEM No.	SOLUTION	EXPLANATION
22	5	The middle number is obtained by subtracting the left hand number from the right hand number, and dividing the result by 2. $28 - 14 = 14 \div 2 = 7$ $25 - 15 = 10 \div 2 = 5.$
23	NOSE	All the others come in pairs.
24	INTER	Which forms the words: winter, sprinter, printer, minter, painter and jointer.
25	2	The figures are symmetrically reversed, both vertically and horizontally. Thus the circle moves from left to right, the bottom square goes to the top and the top square to the bottom.
26	8	The right hand figure is obtained by superimposing the two preceding it and erasing any lines that are common to the first two.
27	CIRCLE (CRICEL)	This is the only geometrical shape amongst parts of the body (HAND, FOOT, THIGH, SHOULDER).
28	12	The sequence is made by subtracting 1 from the

PROBLEM No.	SOLUTION	EXPLANATION

prime numbers in numerical order. Thus $1 - 1 = 0, 3 - 1 = 2, 5 - 1 = 4, 7 - 1 = 6, 11 - 1 = 10, 13 - 1 = 12$.

29   5 The circle and triangle move 90° clockwise each time. The square moves 90° anti-clockwise. The shapes change colour each time.

30   5 The bottom figure on each column is obtained by superimposing the two preceding it, and adding another pattern that is different from the two already there.

31   5/3 The exterior half of each domino is obtained by missing out one number each time, in descending order: 1 (0) 6 (5) 4 (3) 2 (1) 0 (6) 5. On the interior halves, the numbers on the diagonally opposite dominos always add up to 4. Thus: $4 + 0 (= 4)$ 3 $+ 1 (= 4)$ and $1 + 3 (= 4)$.

32   1 It is the only one without an identical pair. Numbers 2 and 3, and 4 and 5, are identical.

PROBLEM No.	SOLUTION	EXPLANATION
33	F	By multiplying together the two numbers preceding each letter, you obtain the position of this letter in the alphabet: $2 \times 2 = $ (D) 4th letter, $3 \times 4 = $ (L) 12th letter, $5 \times 3 = $ (O) 15th letter, $6 \times 1 = $ (F) 6th letter.
34	MERE	The first two letters of the word in brackets are the last two letters of the word to the right; the 3rd and 4th letters are the 4th and 2nd letters of the word on the left.
35	SOLE	Which is a synonym of ONLY and FISH.
36	TAN	Which forms the words CAPSTAN and TANGENT.
37	2	On each line, the right hand figure is obtained by taking the top triangle of the first figure, the bottom triangle of the second figure, and putting them together. The colours are reversed.
38	3	The stripes in the left of the figure turn 45° clockwise each time. The stripes in the right of the figure turn 45° anti-clockwise.

PROBLEM No.	SOLUTION	EXPLANATION
39		In the top triangle, each letter is alphabetically an equal distance from two vowels: (ab) C (de) (ef) G (hi) (ijk) L (mno) (opq) R (stu) (uv) W (xy). The bottom triangle is simply a progression of vowels in the alphabet: A E I O U.
40	16	The second circle contains the numbers in the first circle, divided by 2. The third circle contains the numbers in the first circle multiplied by 2: (4 × 2 =) 8, (6 × 2 =) 12 and (8 × 2 =) 16.

TEST IV: SOLUTIONS

PROBLEM No.	SOLUTION	EXPLANATION
1		1 The horizontal line remains where it is. The other two lines rotate 45° anti-clockwise each time.
2		6 The bottom figure of each column is obtained by superimposing the two preceding figures.
3	**ELM** (MEL)	The only tree amongst a series of flowers: TULIP, CARNATION, PEONY and ROSE.
4		Each number in the top triangle is divided by two and then placed in the lower triangle that follows it. Each number in the lower triangle is multiplied by three and placed in the top triangle that follows it.
5		5 The circle zigzags from left to right; the square moves diagonally downwards from right to left.

PROBLEM No.	SOLUTION	EXPLANATION
6	6	Each figure has one more dot on each of its lines than has the figure on its left.
7	1/1	The ONE alternates between the exterior and interior halves of the dominos. Starting from the interior THREE, the numbers on the other havles progress 4, 5, 6, 0, 1 alternating between the interior and exterior.
8	2	The middle shape stays in the same place but changes colour. The top and bottom shapes swap position.
9	TEN	Which forms the words ROTTEN and TENDON.
10	5	The numbers that come after the roman numerals correspond to the number of lines in that particular roman numeral.
11	MITE	The word in brackets is formed in this way: The 1st letter is the 3rd letter of the left hand word. The 2nd letter is the 3rd letter of the right hand word. The 3rd letter is

PROBLEM No.	SOLUTION	EXPLANATION
		the 5th letter of the left hand word; the 4th letter is the 5th of the right hand word.
12	OVER	Which forms the words: cover, lover, shover, drover, hover, rover, clover, plover, mover.
13	1	On each line the interior circle changes colour each time; the right hand figure's middle ring is a different colour from those of the first two.
14	1	The square, the black circle and the white circle all turn 90° anti-clockwise. The initially black circle changes colour each time.
15		The number inside each triangle is obtained by multiplying together the numbers on each side, and dividing this by the number at the base of the triangle: $3 \times 6 = 18 \div 9 = 2$ $6 \times 4 = 24 \div 8 = 3$ $8 \times 2 = 16 \div 4 = 4$
16		In the top square, each letter is separated from the one that precedes it first by one letter, then 2, then 1, then 2, then 1, then 2. Thus: A (b) C (de) F (g) H (ij) K (l) M (no) P.

PROBLEM No.	SOLUTION	EXPLANATION

In the bottom square, the sequence is:
Y (1st letter before Z)
W (2nd letter before Y)
T (3rd letter before W)
P (4th letter before T)
K (5th letter before P)
E (6th letter before K).

17 2 On each line, the right hand figure is obtained by adding together the two preceding it.

18 4 A and D move one square anti-clockwise each time. B and D move one square clockwise each time.

19 2 On each line, the right hand figure is obtained by superimposing the two preceding it. Any identical exterior triangles cancel each other out.

20 3 All the circles and lines move 45° clockwise each time. The circles are black when in the bottom half of the square, and white when in the top half of the square.

21 SPERM WHALE Wax is to a bee what amber is to a sperm whale.

PROBLEM No.	SOLUTION	EXPLANATION
22	39	The number in brackets is obtained by adding together the two numbers either side and dividing it by 2: $23 + 41 = 64 \div 2 = 32$ $47 + 31 = 78 \div 2 = 39$
23	BRONZE	The only allow amongst a series of metals: copper, tin, lead, iron, aluminium.
24	ASH	Which forms the words: crash, flash, mash, brash, trash, gnash, lash, slash.
25	3	The circle zigzags from top to bottom, while the square moves diagonally upwards from left to right. Both are hidden when they coincide with the black column.
26	8	On each line, the stripes are once horizontal, once vertical and once diagonal. The white and black circles change colour each time.
27	MIDDAY (DAMDIY)	All the others are anagrams of days of the week: Monday, Tuesday, Saturday, Thursday.
28	1	The sequence is $-3, +2$: $6(-3 =) 3(+2 =) 5(-3 =)$ $2(+2 =) 4(-3 =) 1$.

PROBLEM No.	SOLUTION		EXPLANATION

29

6 The initially bottom circle and the triangle move one corner anti-clockwise; the circle changing colour each time. The top circle and the square move one corner clockwise, and also change colour each time.

30

7 On each line the figures are composed of the same three shapes in a different order.

31

2/5 Starting with the domino 6/4, and working anti-clockwise, one half of the dominos follows this sequence: 6 (0) 1 (2) 3 (4) 5 (6) 0 (1) 2. The other half is separated by two numbers each time: 4 (5/6) 0 (1/2) 3 (4/5) 6 (0/1) 2 (3/4) 5.

32

5 The only figure composed of three shapes; all the others are composed of two.

PROBLEM No.	SOLUTION	EXPLANATION
33	1	The letters are those whose position in the alphabet can be found by subtracting the second number from the first, i.e. $4 - 3 = 1$ (A is 1st letter), $5 - 2 = 3$ (C is 3rd letter), $6 - 1 = 5$ (E is 5th letter) $8 - 1 = 7$ (G is 7th letter).
34	GOAL	The word in brackets is obtained in this way: 1st letter is the 3rd letter of the word to the left; 2nd letter is the 2nd letter of the word to the right; 3rd letter is the 4th letter of the word to the right; 4th letter is the 1st letter of the word to the left.
35	JUMPER	A synonym of SWEATER and ATHLETE.
36	LADY	Which makes the words LANDLADY and LADY-BIRD.
37	3	On each line, the top bar is alternately unbroken and broken; the middle bar is the same in the first two figures and then changes in the right hand figure; the bottom bar remains unchanged across each line.

PROBLEM No.	SOLUTION	EXPLANATION
38	4	The top left and bottom right hand squares of each figure make a quarter turn anti-clockwise each time. The top right and bottom left hand squares make a quarter turn clockwise.
39	Y	Y is the next vowel in sequence: A E I O U Y.
40	7	When all three numbers in each line or column are added together, the answer always comes to 24.

YOUR I.Q.

What is your intelligence quotient?

You now have everything you need to calculate your I.Q. Refer to the following table.

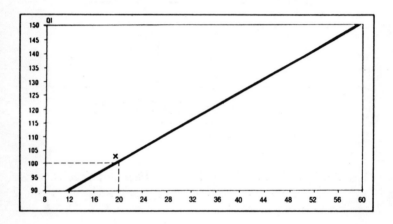

This table allows you to transform your score into an I.Q. To do this you must:

• Add up all the correct answers you obtained in tests 1 and 2;

• Mark this number on the horizontal line of the table;

• Draw a perpendicular up to the diagonal line on the table. This is point X.

• Draw a horizontal from point X to the vertical line on the table. This gives you your I.Q.

• Do the same thing with the answers you obtained in tests 3 and 4 to give you a second I.Q. evaluation.

These two evaluations, which often vary, show you how your intellectual output and your performance can change from one moment to the next during one hour of solid 'work'.

Add your two scores together and divide by two to give you a more realistic indication of your true I.Q.

How you compare

Finally, here is a table devised by Wechsler that you can use to compare your intelligence level with the rest of the population.

I.Q.	Intelligence Level	Percentage of population
130 and above	Very high	2.2%
120 - 129	High	6.7%
110 - 119	Above average	16.1%
90 - 109	Average	50 %
80 - 89	Below average	16.1%
70 - 79	Low	6.7%
60 or below	Deficient	2.2%

• **Between 90 and 110** — You have an average I.Q. Your intelligence is suited to everyday life, and you are easily able to overcome the daily problems life presents.

• **Between 110 and 120** — You are above average; you have an ability to solve problems quickly and efficiently, occasionally showing flashes of brilliance.

• **Between 120 and 130** — You are either particularly on form intellectually at the moment, or very gifted at resolving the sort of problems posed by these tests. A more detailed assessment might be desirable to confirm your performance.

• **Less than 90 and more than 130** — (less than 20 correct answers or more than 42 in two tests). You fall into the categories of 'inferior' and 'highly superior'. The probability that you are one or the other is extremely small. It might be better to admit that this sort of test is not really suitable for evaluating your degree of intelligence.